This workbook BELONGS to

the amazing, INCREDIBLE, scrumptious & ENTIRELY gorgeous

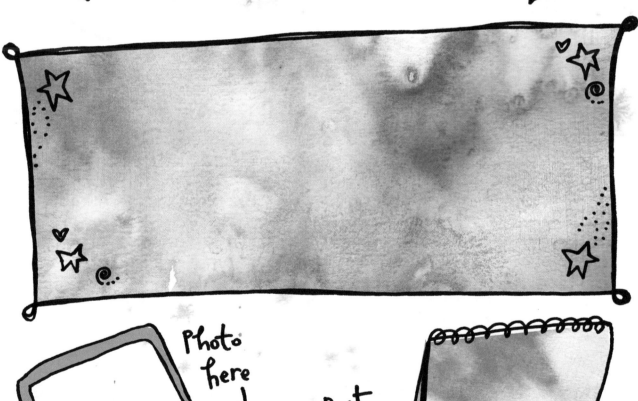

Photo here

Best Contact Details here

We ♡ you:

This book is dedicated to YOU.
Because YOU deserve a shining,
abundant business that sings
to your soul.

We ♡ Paying It Forward:

A portion of roylaties from every book
sold goes to support Kiva and Suluhisho
Children's Village, Kenya.

BenBella Books, Inc.
10440 N. Central Expressway, Suite 800
Dallas, TX 75231
www.benbellabooks.com
Send feedback to
feedback@benbellabooks.com

ISBN: 9781948836111

We ♡ The Internet!:

 FACEBOOK: LeonieDawsonAuthor

WEBSITE: LeonieDawson.com

WEBSITE: ShiningYear.com

The Shining Biz Workbook:
THE SECRET BEHIND BRILLIANT BUSINESSWOMEN!

MUST-HAVE ITEM

"I've been using the workbooks for a few years now. They've allowed me to achieve some really crazy goals I've set for myself. They are a must-have if you want to create an amazing year."

—Denise Duffield-Thomas, Author of *Lucky Bitch*

A GUIDE TO BUILD MY BUSINESS

"Leonie Dawson's workbooks are SO powerful. I have used them every year for the last eight years. I gush about them all the time. Whatever I put in these workbooks ends up becoming destiny. I cannot recommend them enough."

—Hibiscus Moon, Author + Crystal Expert

HIGHLY RECOMMENDED

"I love these workbooks and have used them for years for my life and business. Whatever I write in there ends up happening. I highly recommend them."

—Nathalie Lussier, Entrepreneur, Ambition Ally

TRULY TOOK MY BUSINESS TO THE NEXT LEVEL!

"[This] workbook was the swift kick in the butt I needed to start looking at my business for what it really is, a huge source of joy in my life. Since doing the workbook I have tripled my monthly income and found financial freedom in my business!"

—Flora Sage, Author, Speaker, Coach

PERMISSION TO CREATE A BUSINESS THAT REALLY WAS AUTHENTIC!

"[This] workbook helped me identify what really mattered to me in my business and life, and helped me develop a business that was completely grounded in those values … My business brings me joy and I feel set free from what a person in my industry 'should' look like."

—Katie Cowan, Symphony Law's Founder, Director, Chief Lawyer

I CANNOT TELL YOU THE IMPACT THAT THE WORKBOOK HAD ON MY BUSINESS!

"Leonie's straight-talking, comprehensible approach to business made it easy for me to take all the steps I had either been avoiding or wasn't even aware I should be taking. Within a month I had not only been brave enough to set income targets for the first time, I had met and overshot them!"

—Kate Beddow, Holistic Therapist

EASY + POWERFUL WAY TO TRANSFORM!

"Thanks to Leonie's intuitive and business skills I have grown both in my business and in my personal life. I feel so much more in tune with my needs and I've gained so much clarity. It is so clear to me now that anything is possible. Let the magic begin!"

—Karina Ladet, Intuitive Healer

AMAZED AT THE IMPACT IT HAD!

"Wow! I'm a big forward thinker and straight away this shifted my thinking because first up I had to reflect on the year just past which was incredibly powerful … I ended up purchasing copies for several of my coaching clients so they could enjoy the experience of completing their own workbook too!"

—Belinda Jackson, Marketing, Business + Lifestyle Strategist

I WAS BLOWN AWAY!

"To be honest, I was a bit skeptical when I bought the workbook … However, I was BLOWN AWAY by the value offered … After going through the workbooks, I had a clear plan for achieving both my personal and business goals. I'm now calmer, more focused, and more productive … My monthly income has more than doubled!"

—Shay de Silva, Fitness Coach + Founder of Fast Fitness To Go

G'day Beautiful Soul

Congratulations on choosing this workbook, on stepping up to the plate to making your dreams happen. Congratulations on claiming your role as the Conscious Creator of your own life and business.

Business doesn't have to be hard. It doesn't have to break your finances, your life balance, or your spirit. It can be enormously joyful, profitable, and help thousands of people. It can be a living embodiment of spirit. You CAN have time off. You CAN make glorious amounts of abundance. You CAN live your soul purpose.

What do you need to do to make it happen? You need to dedicate yourself to this work. **Dream** your biggest dream. **Align** your actions with your intentions. **Set your goals** and come back to your goals and **review them**.

(Handy hint: the more you review, the quicker they'll come true!)

But I gotta tell you a secret I've learned over the years of helping women create incredible lives + incredible businesses:

NOT EVERYONE IS READY TO DO THIS WORK. But just the mere fact that you've invested in this workbook sets you apart.

This workbook will take you through the **essential questions** you need to answer in order to shift your business (and life) into something incredible over the next year.

♥Leonie

WARNING!
This workbook creates
CHange...

In late 2009, I had an idea fall into my (pregnant) lap.

Make a workbook for your New Year's resolutions, the idea whispered. *Write out your dreams. Find out what happens when you dream your big dream and commit it to words.*

Ever faithful to ideas that fall into laps, I did. And then it whispered: *Share it with the world. More people need it than just you.*

And so I did. I thought it might be helpful to maybe ten others. That would make me happy—ten lives changed. Ten lives did get changed. I didn't anticipate, however, that it would go on to become an instant hit. Not only that, it started making miracles.

Changing lives. Making dreams happen. Since then, over 300,000 women have created their own shining biz + life using this workbook.

It works. Like crazy.

So dearest, are you ready?

Ready for the ginormous, glorious change that is coming?

Your Shining Year is waiting for YOU!

Results *you* should SEE *from using the Workbooks?*

Increased income

Increased audience

Reach your business goals faster

Better work-life balance

Increased self-confidence

More clarity in direction for biz AND life

Discover likeminded biz soul sisters!

Get the support and team you need

Have your best year yet in business

→ INSERT YOUR DREAM HERE ↘ ←
The result I want to see is...

_____

Why is it so IMPORTANT to set & review goals?

When you don't get clarity around where you've been + where you want to go, you can get stuck in the same old place + same old routine.

YOU NEED:

⭐ To spend time dreaming up your vision

⭐ To let go of all the old past stuff + be grateful for it so you can move onward

⭐ Support systems to help you make it happen

⭐ Delicious, probing questions to help you get to the soul of what it is you need

⭐ To review your goals regularly so you can take ACTION + bring them into the world!

A goal without a PLAN is just a wish

Want to be in the top (1%) of achievers?*

16% don't write down

4% write down

80% of people do not even THINK of goals

1% write goals down & regularly REVIEW. They are among the HIGHEST ACHIEVERS

Use this workbook as a guide to help you map out your year in biz—so you can make miracles this year!

How to USE this Workbook!

This workbook works, IF you fill it out.

Set a deadline for yourself to get it done, and then give yourself the time you need.

Don't give up if January is over!

It's only too late to plan if you don't ever fill it out!

Make sure you put it in your calendar to review your workbook regularly to keep you on track—I do it monthly for myself. The more you review it, the more your goals will come true!

Use the Monthly Check-in Pages at the end of this book to help you review your goals regularly.

Set deadlines for each of your goals. Set MORE deadlines for each step of your goals. Make sure you put them into your calendar too, then DO THEM.

Aim to make your workbook dog-eared, well-thumbed, and deeply familiar. It is your companion and guide for making your life and biz SHINE!

IMPORTANT REMINDER: Do what you can. Invest time in your beautiful dreams. Surround yourself with supportive souls. You CAN do this!

THE
VERY IMPORTANT

2018

Closing Ceremony

Celebrating & Releasing 2018

Here's the place where we muck it up

We set our NEW resolutions, our NEW goals, our NEW dreams… without ever taking stock of where we are NOW in our businesses and lives.

I'm always surprised at how little clarity business owners have of where their businesses are at right now—their finances, customer base, achievements, and challenges. It's almost like they feel afraid to look. And yet when we peer into the dark, we can shine a light on exactly where we are right now, and where we need to head. It's incredibly useful + powerful.

I promise you, it doesn't have to be scary! In fact, it can be FUN!

Put your Fun Underoos on!

I promise you, this closing ceremony will earn you the most amount of abundance + impending goodness if you do it. Be gentle with you. Trust the process. These questions will bring you a huge surge of clarity that can be incredibly powerful.

Celebrating & Releasing 2018

You've been sent here on a mission.

To discover every part of yourself. To grow wiser than you ever thought possible. To find the light even in the darkest cave.

2018 happened to you the way it did for a reason. Sometimes there are reasons you cannot possibly begin to know right now. At other times the reason + the blessing is easy to see. Even when it's hard, it doesn't mean it wasn't meant to happen. It's all taking you to where you need to go.

You are getting braver, deeper, wiser, more beautiful by the moment, by the day, by the year.

Let's celebrate + release 2018.

And clear the pathway for the miracles to come.

I choose freeDom. I choose strength. I choose laughter + courage.

What are your BIZ accomplishments over the past year?
(Fill the page—they can be big or small! They are
ALL important!)

What business dreams
came true during 2018?

What were your business weak points?
What do you know needs to improve?

What challenges and blessings
did you have with customer service this year?

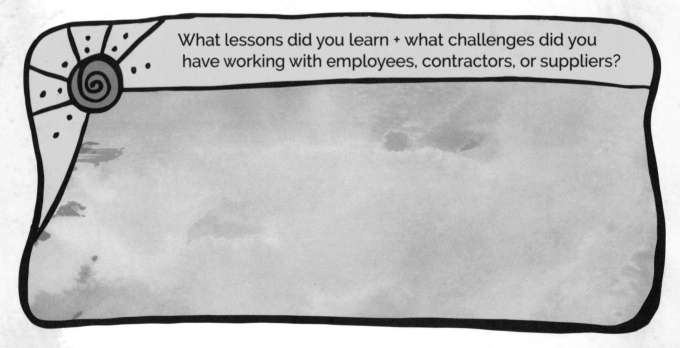

What lessons did you learn + what challenges did you
have working with employees, contractors, or suppliers?

👁 am a DEVOTEE of my dreams + a
GODDESS of my goals.

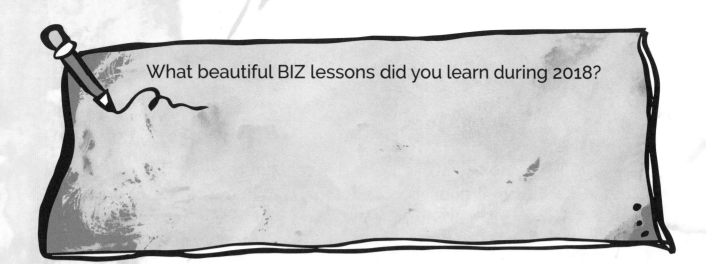

What beautiful BIZ lessons did you learn during 2018?

What were the areas that felt out of whack, hard to follow, or crazy-making in your business this year?
What could be done to change them?

Okay. Are you ready, love? It's time to LOOK at MONEY!

We often avoid looking at real figures—and yet it is tremendously powerful for us to know our numbers so we can GROW them. You can do this, love. (This page will earn you more money than any other.)

Yes, it really IS that important + powerful!

What was your total revenue for 2018? (i.e. what was the total amount of money that came into the business?)

What were your total expenses for 2018?

What was your net profit for 2018 (i.e. total income minus expenses)?

Create a pie chart of your expenses + profit levels:

Important note: do not get discouraged by these numbers. They are not the numeric value of your worth or dream. They are just numbers. Numbers that can grow as soon as we know where we are growing from!

WHAT WERE YOUR ⑤ BEST-SELLING PRODUCTS/SERVICES IN 2018?

Name of Offering:	How much it earned:
①	
②	
3.	
4	
5.	

Create a **PIE CHART** of how YOUR PRODUCTS/SERVICES Sold!

Handy tip: Doing this will give you a HUGE amount of clarity + earn you a butt-load more moolah!

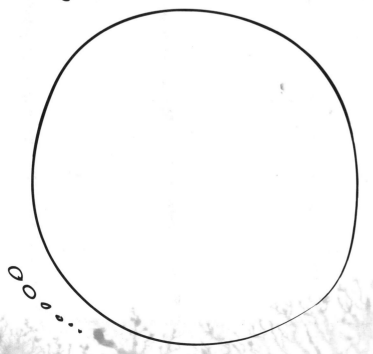

What insights did you get out of this exercise?

HOW MUCH DID YOUR TRIBE GROW IN 2018?

PLATFORM	CURRENT #	HOW MUCH DID THAT # INCREASE?
Email List		
Facebook		
Twitter		
YouTube		
Instagram		

ADD YOUR OWN HERE

What marketing WORKED for you this year?
What created wins for you?

How many days off did you take in the last year?

What was the worst thing about your business in 2018?

What did you learn from this?

What was the best thing about your business in 2018?

What did you learn from this?

What do you need to write, journal, or rant about in order for you to feel clear about 2018 in your business?

A page of gratitude. Draw, write, illustrate, post pictures of EVERYTHING you are grateful for in your biz from 2018!

Completion Circle

(place your hand in the circle to receive the energy)

We breathe & give thanks for all that has passed...

We open up to the beautiful possibilities blossoming before us...

We let go & breathe, releasing all that's old & no longer serves us...

We radiate in light & joy... all is beautiful & all is well...

Invoking 2019

It's time to dream a new dream.

Time to create an incredible year for yourself, your world, your life, the world.

First comes the THOUGHT.

Then the WORD.

Then the ACTION.

That's how change happens.

are you ready?

YES   NO

MY
Shining
2019

INVOKING
THE YEAR AHEAD

MY Shining Finances

WHAT ARE YOUR INCOME GOALS FOR 2019?

Revenue	
Expenses	
Profit!	

USE THE FOLLOWING PAGES TO HELP YOU BRAINSTORM THE DETAILS!

Expenses Budgeting

YOUR SALARY	
STAFF	
RENT	
EQUIPMENT	
SOFTWARE	
WEBSITE DESIGN/ HOSTING	

ADD YOUR OWN HERE

Play around with different sales numbers for different product combinations to see what feels like the right fit for you.

PRODUCT	PRICE	#SOLD	Total

grand Total →

Do you have the right bookkeeper or accountant to support your business financially?

YES NO

How much do you currently have in business savings?

How much do you need in order to pay tax obligations?

Do you need credit cards or loans for your business to help with cash flow as you grow?

YES NO

What passive income will you create?

Calculate Your Company's Net Worth

Dearest: please note that this is not for working out your personal net worth. Do that in your Shining Life workbook! This is for your business as an entity and it's important to start looking at your net worth + the company's net worth as separate.

Assets	$ Worth
Equipment	
Stock	
TOTAL ASSETS	
Liabilities	$ Cost
Credit Cards	
Loans	
TOTAL LIABILITIES	
NET WORTH (ASSETS MINUS LIABILITIES)	

ADD YOUR OWN HERE

How to be a great money custodian...

Circle how you want to develop your fiscal ($) powers this year....

+ HAVE FUN COLORING IN!!

PAY off all DEBT

Read a MONEY book

Learn about STOCKS

Learn about Real Estate

MAKE a BUDGET

TRACK MONEY

Find a GREAT ACCOUNTANT OR BOOK-KEEPER

Mint.com

TRY an online money management system

Find + consolidate Super/ retirement accounts

WORK ON YOUR MONEY BLOCKS

ADD YOUR OWN HERE

ADD YOUR OWN HERE

MONEY resources!

+ HAVE FUN COLORING IN!!

BAREFOOT INVESTOR — Scott Pape

Get RICH, Lucky Bitch ♥ DENISE DUFFIELD-THOMAS

SECRETS OF... THE Millionaire Mind ☆ T. HARV ECKER

ONE MINUTE Millionaire • ALLEN + HANSEN

THE Millionaire NEXt door • T.J. Stanley

Retire Young Retire Rich ★ ROBERT KIYOSAKI

Abundance ☆ P. Diamandis

It's not about the MONEY ♥ BOB PROCTOR

It's RISING TIME! ✳ Kim Kiyosaki

HOW Rich People think S. SIEBOLD

THE RICHEST MAN IN BABYLON G.S. Clason

Be a shining custodian of money

MONEY & MANIFESTING WORKSHOP

LEONIE'S SIMPLE Money Planner

7 LIFE CHANGING HABITS FOR AN ABUNDANT YEAR

More Shining Money Resources from Leonie at SHININGACADEMY.COM

My Shining Team:

Do you have the team you need? **YES** **NO**

What's working well with your team right now?

What's not working well? How can you improve it?

What roles
do you need to
fill this year?

What additional support do you need from your team?

What is keeping you from growing your team?

Do you have the contractors you need?

YES **NO**

What's working well with your contractors right now?

What's not working well? How can you improve it?

Do you have the suppliers you need?

Brainstorm how you could make an even better working relationship with suppliers:

TEAM recommended Resources

Top grading ▽ B.SMART

DELIVERING HAPPINESS ♡ Tony Hseih

PEAK * Chip Conley

NO B.S. TIME Management for Entrepreneurs D. KENNEDY

The Entrepreneur's Guide to Getting Your Shit DONE J. CARLTON

THE E-MYTH REVISITED Michael E. Gerber

SCALING UP Verne Harnish

My Shining Support

Do you have a mentor you can turn to?

Have you outgrown your mentor?

Do you have a mastermind* of people you can brainstorm with and receive advice from?

Are you using it actively enough?

Have you outgrown your mastermind*?

Do you have enough support with childcare?

Do you have an office/studio/working space that will help your business grow?

Brainstorm ways you can create or find a mastermind* that supports you:

*A mastermind is a group of people who meet—either online or in real life—to encourage and support each others' business and/or personal growth.]

How can you go closer and deeper with the mastermind you have?

Who is your ideal mastermind or accountability partner?

What kind of mentor(s) do you need for the next year?

Brainstorm ways you can receive more childcare support:

What do you need in order to thrive as a CEO over the next year?

Who can you go to when things suck and you just need to moan?

My Shining Systems...

It's time to check how strong your systems are!

First, a quick note: What do we mean when we say "SYSTEMS"?

Systems are what your business is built on. It's how things are done. Your procedures. How you run your team. What technology you use to run your business. How each task is executed.

Systems are the things that help our business grow beyond our own workload. To learn more about systems and how to create them, head to the resources section at the end of this chapter!

Use this checklist to see what systems you have in place and what you need to work on. Add your actionables to your systems notes pages at the end of this chapter to work on over the year.

By the end of 2019, your systems will have grown stronger than ever to support you and your business growth!

SOPs

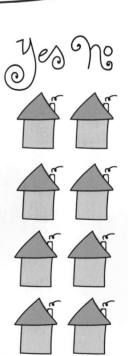

Do you have Standard Operating Procedures (SOPs)?

Do you have a system for updating your SOPs constantly + keeping them updated?

Do you do regular reviews of your SOPs?

Are your staff trained in all your systems?

Accounting systems

Yes   No

Is your accounting system robust enough?

Can you easily access statistics on how much income, expenses, and taxes your business is generating?

Do you know when you need to submit your taxes?

Do you know what you need to do in order to submit your taxes?

Do you have a central place for invoices and receipts (both physical and digital)?

Is your business ready for an audit?

Organization systems

Yes   No

Do you have a filing system for all your digital documents, photographs, and files?

Do you have a physical filing system that works?

Do you have a system for organizing + following up on all incoming snail mail?

Do you have a system for organizing + following up on all important email?

Do you have critical documents and information backed up?

Do you have a system for making sure they are backed up regularly (i.e. monthly)?

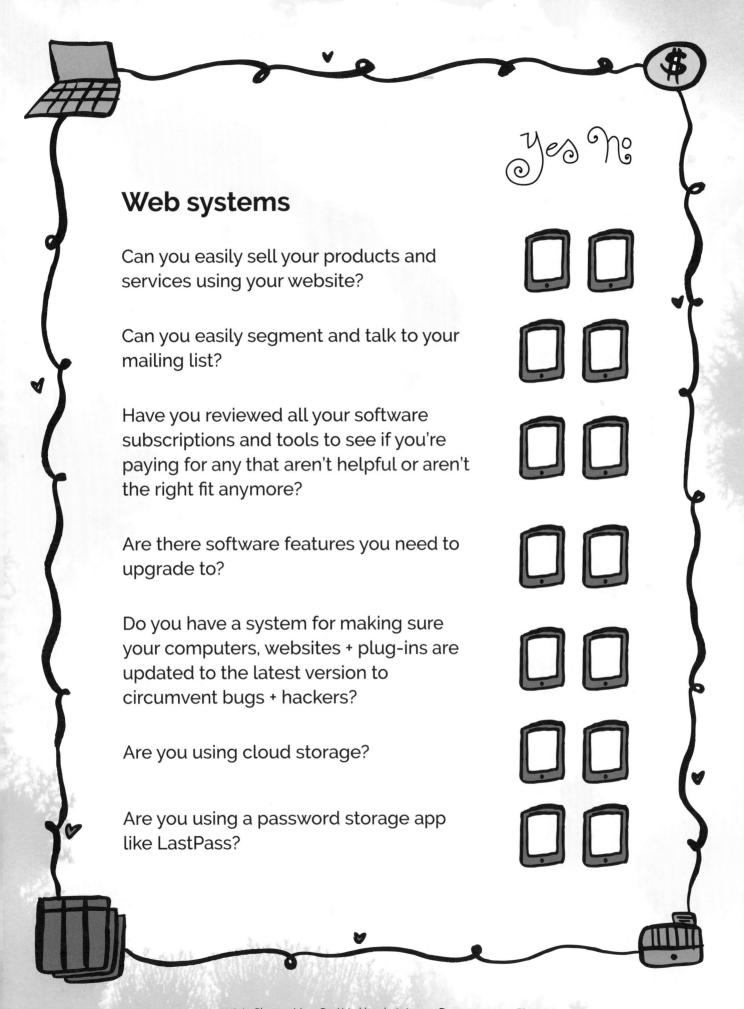

Web systems

Yes No

Can you easily sell your products and services using your website?

Can you easily segment and talk to your mailing list?

Have you reviewed all your software subscriptions and tools to see if you're paying for any that aren't helpful or aren't the right fit anymore?

Are there software features you need to upgrade to?

Do you have a system for making sure your computers, websites + plug-ins are updated to the latest version to circumvent bugs + hackers?

Are you using cloud storage?

Are you using a password storage app like LastPass?

Legal systems

YES no

Do you have all the business registrations you need?

Do you have the right business or company structure set up?

Do you need an Exit Strategy?

Do you have a written plan for your business if you (or your business partner) suffer from illness, accident, or (gawd forbid!) death?

Does anyone else (besides you) know where that written plan is?

Do you have all the insurances you need?

Customer systems

YES no

Do you have a system to ensure all customer support emails and calls are answered/returned efficiently?

Are your customers taken care of beautifully in all areas of your business?

Are you capturing customer data so you can keep in conversation with them?

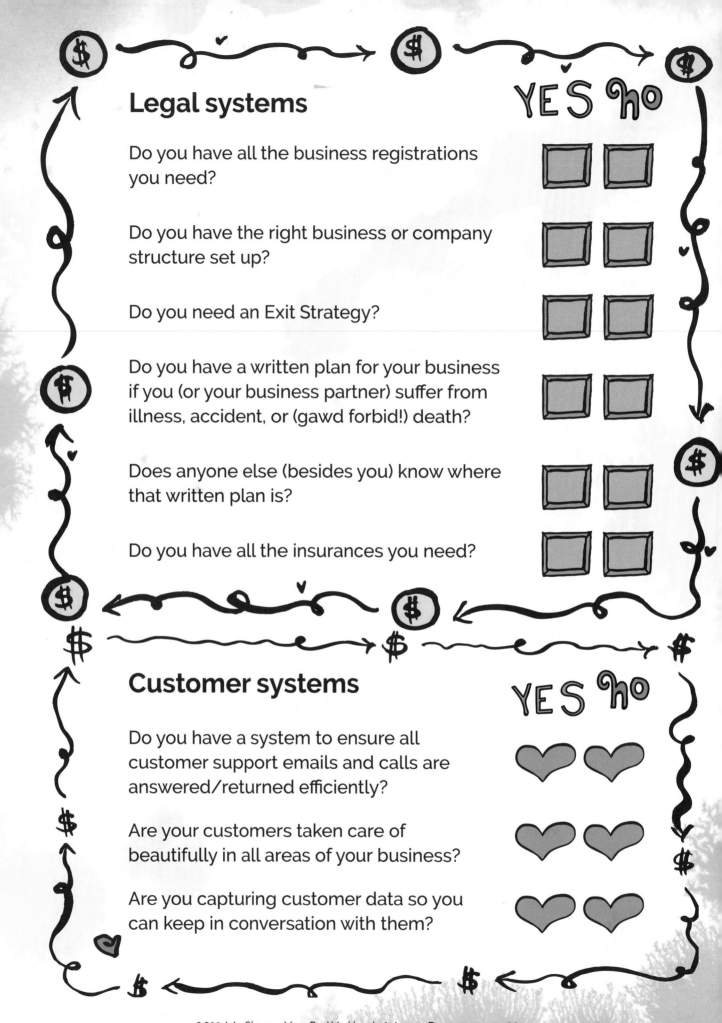

General systems

Yes No

Are there places you're bursting at the
seams and afraid of what growth might
do to your business?

Can you build the customer
experiences you want to or are you
limited by your technology?

Do you have support resources in place
for all critical systems?

Are there places in your business that
are running on a whisper and a prayer?

Do you have systems that need to
be upgraded now you have higher
volume?

Are your systems freeing you up to do
what you do best?

Are you supported in the areas that are
difficult or time-consuming?

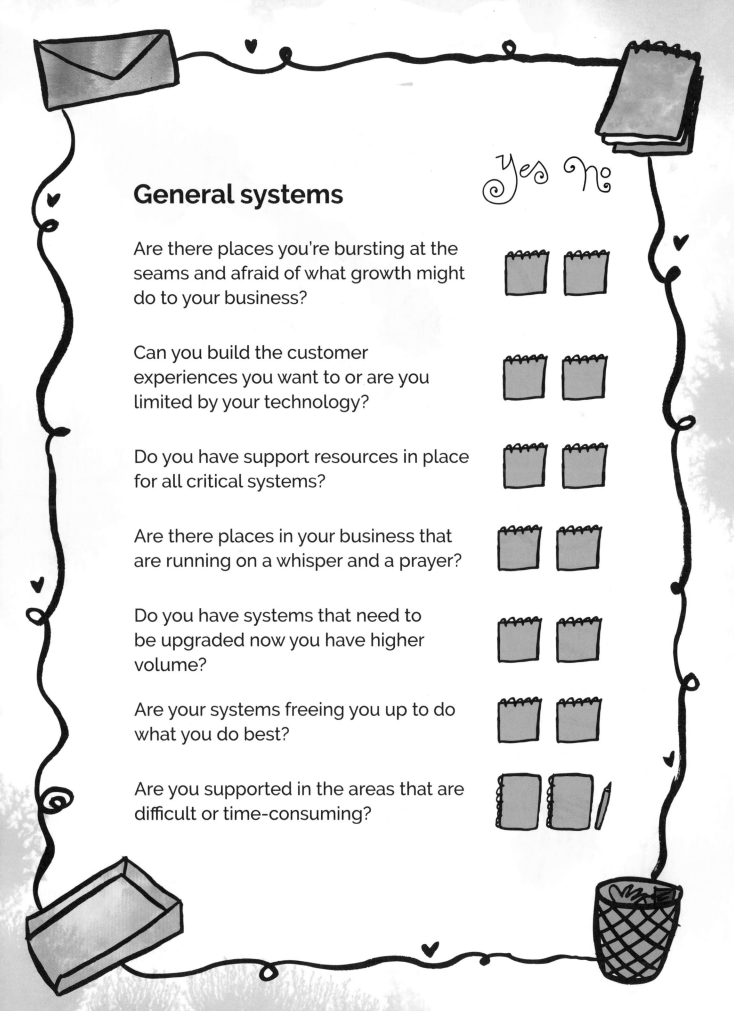

SYSTEMS RECOMMENDED RESOURCES

+ HAVE FUN COLORING IN!!

THE entrepreneur's TRAP
T. FORSYTH

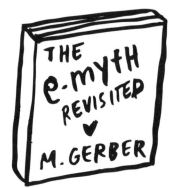

THE e-myth REVISITED ♥ M. GERBER

SCALING UP Verne Harnish

DOUBLE DOUBLE Cameron Herold

How to create ▶ Your S.O.P's

Sneak peek ▶ into LDI S.O.P's

SHININGACADEMY.COM

My Shining Boundaries & Balance

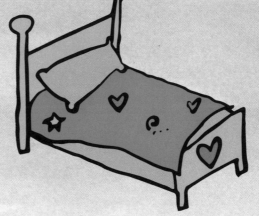

THIS YEAR  GIVE MYSELF PERMISSION in MY BIZ TO...

Permission Slip

Taking holidays is ridunkulously important for your mental vibrance, work/life balance, and your joy for life. How many holidays will you take this year?

When?

What do you need to do to make them happen?

WHAT Self Care RULES WILL I HAVE?

+ HAVE FUN COLORING IN!!

NO WORKING AT NIGHT

NO WORK ON
Adventure Rest
Saturday Sunday
WEEKENDS

GO TO BED
EARLY

NO PHONES IN BEDROOM

add your own:

I WILL ONLY WORK ___ HOURS A WEEK

MONTHLY SPA AFTERNOONS

READ NON-BIZ BOOKS ON WEEKENDS!

Times/Days that ARE WORK-FREE:

BUY + WEAR A BADGE LIKE this?

get a LIFE!

I WILL LIMIT LIVE EVENTS/NETWORKING TO ONLY:

A MONTH/YEAR

Let's get your TIME Sorted!

HOW I CURRENTLY SPEND MY TIME!

Create a pie chart of how your life balance currently looks in the mixup of biz, life, fun, rest + work.

HOW I WANT TO SPEND MY TIME!

Create a pie chart of how you want to create balance in all areas of your biz, life, family, friendships + hobbies!

Make boundaries your besties!

Stop! HAMMER TIME!

So you want to start creating NEW things, yeah?

To do that, you're going to need to clear out the OLD. You need to get rid of old activities, thoughts + habits that aren't helping you move forward. Maybe they once did, but no longer.

What are you going to STOP doing in your biz this year?

CREATE YOUR OWN
My Shining Habits
LIST

What joyful + nourishing habits would you like to cultivate during 2019? Don't worry about how hard it is to form habits—what we'll do instead is create a poster to remind ourselves each day of the beautiful things we'd like to do.

Some days we might do all of them, most days we'll only get to some … other days we may not get to any of them. All of this is gorgeous + fine.

It's not about perfection or failure. What it's about is reminding ourselves of the sacred toolkit of activities we have available to us.

Brainstorm what amazing habits you'd like to include + create your own poster. I've included a blank one you can fill out + two examples you can draw inspiration from. You can do it!

THINGS TO THINK ABOUT WHEN CREATING

My Shining Habits

 Make them sound like fun. Use words that lift you + get you excited to do it.

 Make your habits feel achievable. On my list I say to move for 5 minutes—even though I almost always do way more. If I wrote it down as moving for 15 minutes, it would sound like too much for me + I would avoid it like crazy. Make it achievable so when you do get it done, you'll feel that gorgeous sense of HURRAH + will continue making habits happen in your day. Any extra you do will be a bountiful bonus!

 Phrase them positively as something to move toward instead of being a "Don't."

 Copy habits that sing to you + listen to your spirit to hear what it needs.

There is a WISE WOMAN inside you that KNOWS the way...

ZEN Habits

1. Set your 3 <u>M.I.T.'s</u> at the start of each work session
   <u>Most Important Tasks</u>

2. Whenever you FEEL DiSheveLeD → Declutter

3) "move a muscle to move a mood" —Julia Cameron

4. Keep a gRatitude journal

5. Eat GREEN THINGS or have a GREEN Smoothie

6. Have a TECH FREE bedroom

7. Take | Sabbath

8. Or Monofocus

From Leo Babauta at ZenHabits.net

My Shining Habits

BRiLLiANCE + STAR DUST!

My Shining Education

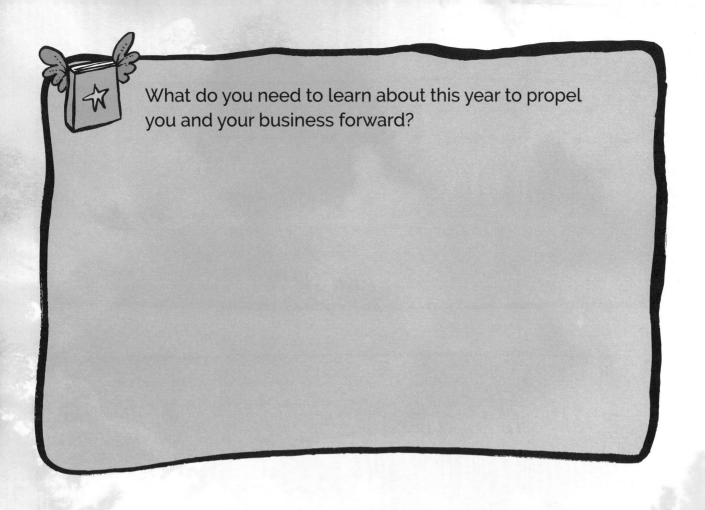

What do you need to learn about this year to propel you and your business forward?

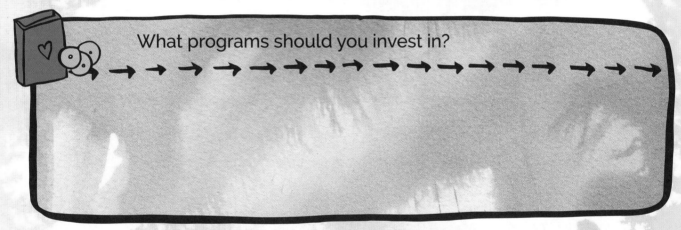

What programs should you invest in?

→ → → → → → → → → → → → → → → → → →

What books do you want to read this year?

→ → → → → → → → → → → → → → → → → →

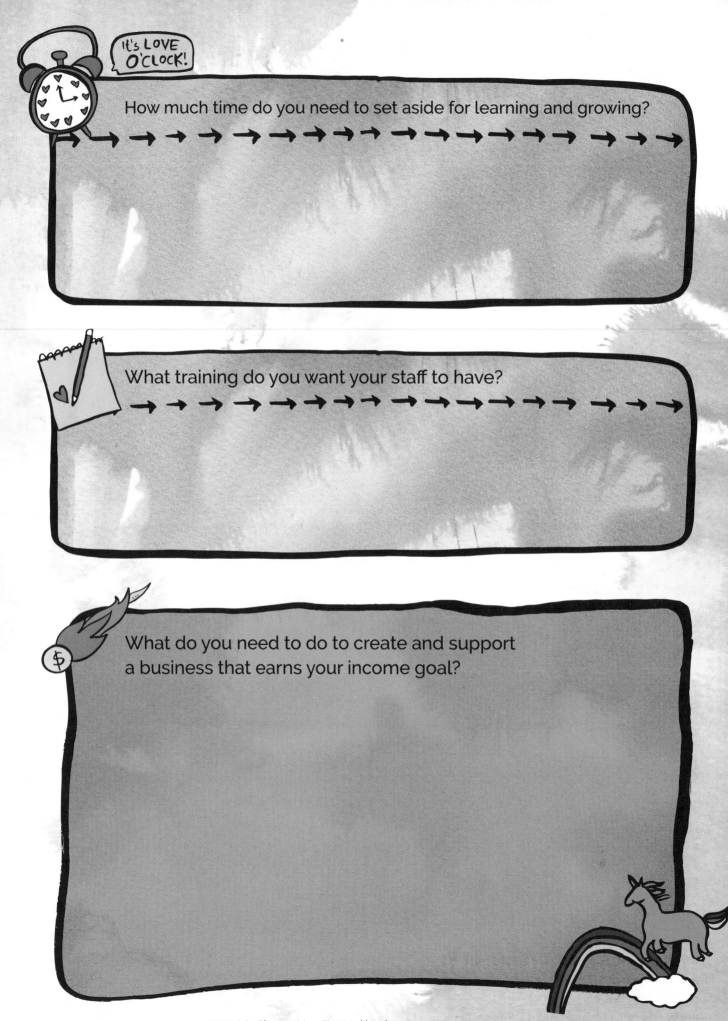

It's LOVE O'CLOCK!

How much time do you need to set aside for learning and growing?

What training do you want your staff to have?

What do you need to do to create and support a business that earns your income goal?

EDUCATION — RECOMMENDED RESOURCES! ☆

Good to Great
J. COLLINS

Scaling Up
Verne Harnish

Delivering Happiness ☆
Tony Hseih

FOUR HOUR WORK WEEK
T Ferriss

E-MYTH REVISITED ♥
M.E GERBER

How could you improve your customer support this year?

Where do your customers get "stuck" the most?
What could you do to stop them from getting stuck
in the first place?

How can you reward your most loyal customers?

How can you capture more of your customers' testimonials and success stories?

Don't let the Big Overwhelm of Everything stop you from starting right now!

Customer Love Day

A gorgeous yearly ritual we like to do at Leonie Dawson International is have a yearly Customer Love Day, where we do something special for our customers to show them just how much we appreciate them.

You can hold a party, run a free workshop, make thank you phone calls, send out thank you postcards, have a sale for loyal clients, send gifts to your biggest or most loyal clients.

Consider creating a Customer Love Day for your business. Brainstorm ideas now of what you could do to celebrate the incredible tribe of people that your business serves. And schedule your own day in!

WHEN? SCHEDULE IT IN!

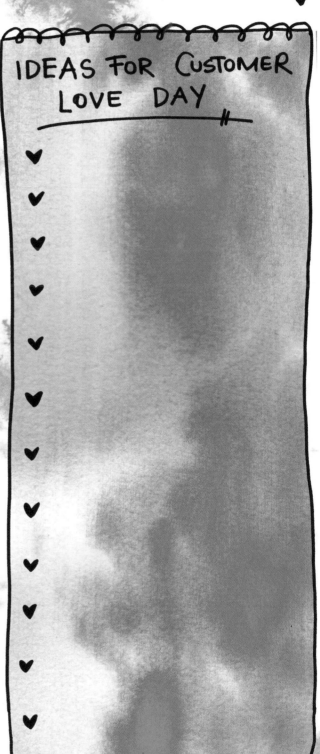

IDEAS FOR CUSTOMER LOVE DAY

My Shining marketing

How much will 👁 extend the [Reach →] of my business this year?

Platform	HOW BIG WILL IT BE BY END OF 2019?
✉ Mailing List	
f Facebook	
t Twitter	
. . . .	
. . . .	
. . . .	
. . . .	

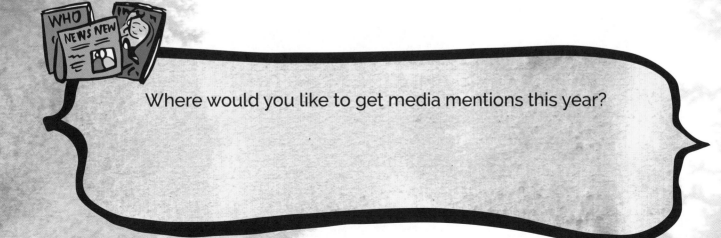

Where would you like to get media mentions this year?

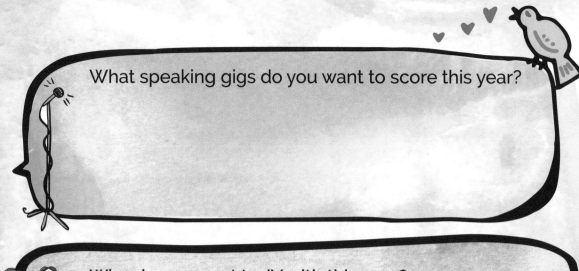

What speaking gigs do you want to score this year?

Who do you want to JV with this year?

JV = Joint Venture

When you team up with someone to cocreate + sell a product/service together. They might have the same target customer as you, but offer something different to what you do.

What networking events do you want to attend this year?

Testimonials: how many do you want to gather this year? How will you do this?

What will I CREATE this year?

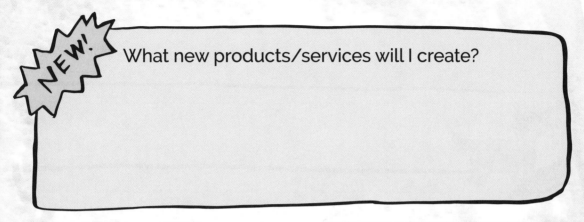

NEW!

What new products/services will I create?

How many blog posts will I create this year?

_____

`A` `∞` `✎` `</>`   SAVE   PUBLISH

How many newspaper articles will I submit this year?

WHERE TO?

_____
_____

File Edit View Bookmarks

How many ezines OR NEWSletters will I send this year?

Subscribe

FREE!

What free opt-in offers will you create this year?

What other goals do you want to make for your business this year?

RECOMMENDED RESOURCES FOR *Marketing*

SHARE YOUR WORK
• A. Kleon

CASHVERTISING
D.E. Whitman

SHARK TALES
Barbara Corcoran

WORDS that SELL
R. BAYAN

INFLUENCE
R. Cialdini

Content Rules ☆
Handley + Chapman

MY Shining World

How much money do you want your business to donate this year?

To which cause(s)?

How do you want to donate your services or time this year? To where?

What ways can your business reduce its environmental impact this year?

How can your business make a positive impact on the world?

How can your business help your local community this year?

Have you undertaken the free B-Corp assessment?

YES   NO

BCorporation.net

Community Resources

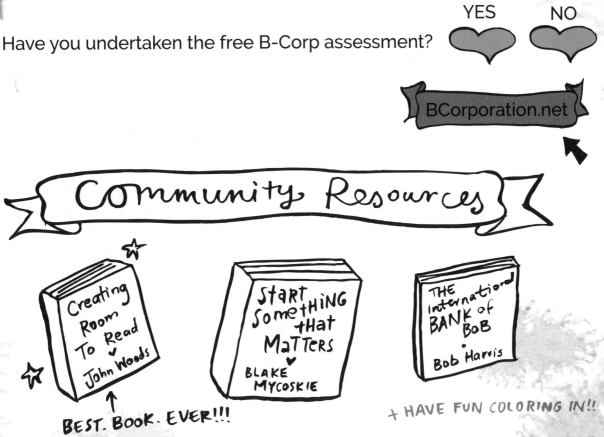

Creating Room To Read ♥ John Woods

BEST. BOOK. EVER!!!

Start Something that Matters BLAKE MYCOSKIE

THE International BANK of BOB Bob Harris

+ HAVE FUN COLORING IN!!

MY Shining Dreams

ROUNDING IT ALL UP

My goals that are so big and daring that
I'm not even sure they are possible are...

100 things to do in 2019

Dream up 100 glorious goals for you to do in your business this year.
Either make this the master list of all your goals, or stretch your mind
to think what else is possible. Big or small, it doesn't matter.
Just get your pen writing!

1.

2.

3.

4.

5.

6.

7.

{8}

IX.

10.

11.

12.

13.

14.

15.

16.

17.

18.

19.

20.

21.

22.

23.

{24}

25.

26.

27.

28.

29.

30.

30.

32.

33

34

35.

36

37

38.

39

40

41.

42

43

44

45

46

47.

48

49.

50.

51

52.

53.

54.

55.

56

57

58

59.

60

61.

62.

63.

64.

65.

66.

67.

68.

69.

70.

71.

72.

{73.}

74.

75.

[76]

77.

(78.)

79.

80.

YOU CAN DO THIS.

81.

82.

83.

84.

85.

86.

87.

88.

89.

90.

91.

[92]

93.

94.

95.

96.

{97}

98.

99

100.

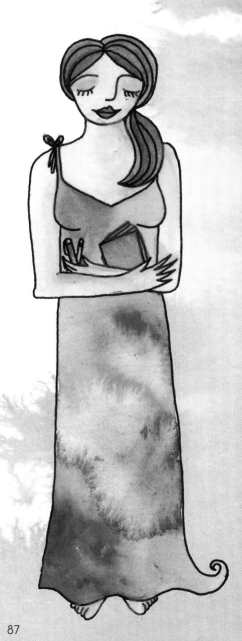

My Dreamiest Day

I wish this was an assignment we were given in school. I wish we'd been taught how to dream big, and create the life we wanted. At least we're making up for it now, hey, lovely?

I want you to write in as much DETAIL as possible your DREAM DAY. Let's talk about your dreamiest day. Where would you be? Who would you be with? What would you do?

I promise you, this is powerful! It's time to become an expert in yourself and your dreams!

2019 Oracle Reading :)

I began giving myself "yearly forecast" oracle readings in 2011.

I just scrawled down the themes on a piece of paper.

my 2011 card reading... amazingly accurate

It amazed me as I referred back to it each month how accurate + helpful it had been.

And it was so beautiful + useful when it came to preparing for what was to come too!

You can do the same—and you don't have to use oracle cards! You can use tarot, angel cards, holy texts like the Bible or Quran, sacred poetry books, or any other gorgeous cards or books that call to your spirit.

Just sit with your intention to create a space of guidance and inspiration for yourself, connect to your own shining spirit, and then give yourself your reading for each month of the year ahead.

I used Lucy Cavendish's "Oracle of the Dragonfae" for my reading.

They are my favorite cards to do readings with—they have become like dear friends to me!

TinyURL.com/DragonfaeCards

There are so many oracle + tarot cards out there that you can use. Choose the one that calls to your heart.

For a list of some of my other favorite oracle cards, head to:

TinyURL.com/LeonieTopOracles

GIVE YOURSELF AN

Oracle Reading

FOR THE YEAR

Pull 12 oracle or tarot cards for your year ahead. If you prefer, you can also randomly choose passages from a holy book, create prayers, randomly choose lyrics, or whatever sings to your spirit! There is no wrong way to do this!

Ask your angels, guides, or God (whoever you resonate with most) to give you any messages you need to help you shine in 2019.

If you don't have your own cards, try an online oracle …
I ♥ Joanna Powell Colbert at GaianTarot.com

Write down the card messages for each month …
just go with the words that feel the most important.

2019 Oracle Reading:

January

February

March

April

2019 Oracle Reading

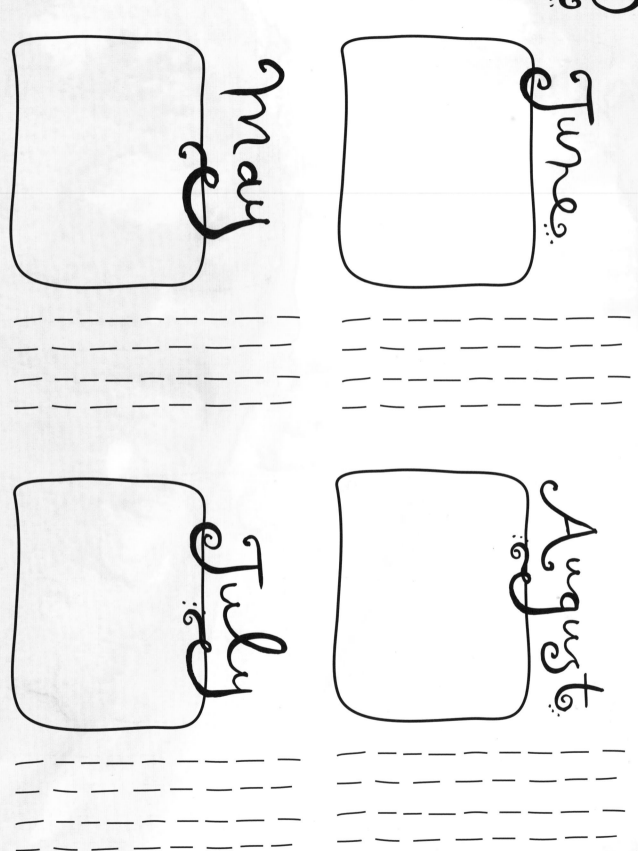

May

June

July

August

2019 Oracle Reading

September

October

November

December

CREATE A  Dreamboard FOR 2019

Dreamboards are an incredibly powerful tool for drawing your dreams to you through the Law of Attraction. Not only that, they serve as visual guideposts that are not only beautiful and inspiring to look at, but will help you remember every.single.day. your dreams + highest intentions for this year.

And as we all know, what we focus on becomes true. Creating your very own dreamboard right now will help seal the deal between you and your dreams!

Supplies you will need:

A piece of cardboard, thick paper, OR canvas in whatever size feels RIGHT To you.

Glue

Scissors

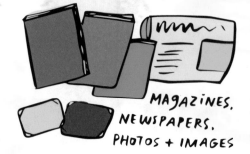
MAGAZINES, NEWSPAPERS, PHOTOS + IMAGES

A little blend of OPENNESS, COURAGE, JOY + A SPRINKLE OF HOPE. ☆ ♡ ☺ ☽

CREATE A Dreamboard FOR 2019

Search through MAGAZINES for images + words of things, people, experiences + feelings we'd like to draw into our lives for the next year ♥ ♥ ♥

Cut out images that lift you up, inspire you & make you feel Radiant ★ IGNORE all images + words that feel like a SHOULD.

glue them onto your CARDBOARD until it feels ≥ just RIGHT ≤ to your spirit ♥

PLACE it SOMEWHERE YOU SEE it DAILY. ON YOUR desk, BY YOUR BED, even on the back of your door!

♥ YOU CAN ALSO USE THE FOLLOWING PAGE TO CREATE A MINI PORTABLE DREAMBOARD TO KEEP WITH YOUR WORKBOOK!

Ⓟ You can also use Pinterest as an ONLINE DREAMBOARD. You might also like to create a companion Pinterest board for dreams fulfilled too!

& watch it magically appear!

MY MINI PORTABLE
dreamboard

Dreamboard EXAMPLES

LeonieDawson.com/Dreamboard

THE LIST OF Things To Do WHEN EVERYTHING SUCKS!

Our feelings can change in an instant. Fickle things they are—generated by the moment, the situation, our hormones + our perspective. If we can change just one of these things, a great healing can occur.

We can go from rock bottom to, "You know what? I'm okay…" in about 15 minutes. There's a world of difference between those 2 places. All we need to do is remember the things that work for us…the little changes that can make a big difference.

Let's prepare ourselves now… let's write our reminder list of Things To Do When Everything Sucks.

My list to de-suckify

★ go outside for 5 minutes

★ smell lavender

★ get sunshine on my face

★ eat something green

★ have a shower

★ do a 5-minute meditation or breather

> Cut this out + put it in a place you can grab in case of sucktastic emergency… purse, desk, or type it into your phone

SURE! Cut me out, ♥ love!

In case the suckies strike

1
2
3
4
5
6
7
8
9
10

How my company turns our GOALS into ACTION

Set a **DEADLINE** to finish workbook

Get copies made for everyone on team ♥ ♥ ♥ ♥

Set QUARTERLY GOALS. Lay out BIG PROJECTS on wall planner.

PROJECT PLAN it!

- Pile all the goals + activities into our project management software

DRILL down to details — every single task that needs to be done to complete goal

Assign everything to WHO will do it!

Have <u>deadlines</u> + <u>due</u> dates for everything

REVIEW + CHECK ON PROGRESS *Monthly*

Make youR GOALS happen!

Setting your goals is just one part of the process of making things happen.

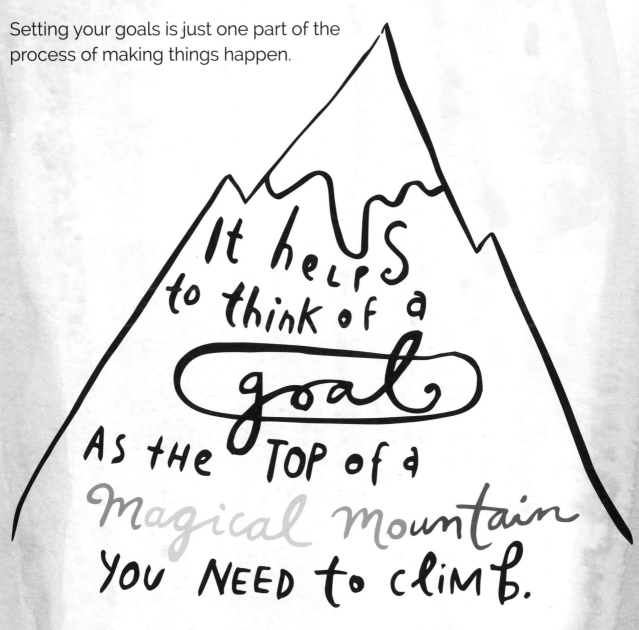

It helps to think of a goal as the TOP of a magical mountain YOU NEED to climb.

Getting to the top (the goal!) is not possible with just one step!

You're going to need to climb that mountain one step at a time.

And sometimes, there will be some steps that need other things done to complete them too—which can feel overwhelming, and like the top will never be reached.

Mount Creative

Once you have your goal, brainstorm all of the things that you need to do to get there.

List all the tiny steps that have to happen before you get to the top. STOP! Don't overthink this! Just get them down.

SUPER tip*

If your step has more than 1 piece, separate them into 2 steps.

The really wonderful thing is this: the more you hone your steps into smaller pieces, the more focused you become, because the thinking is already done. You just get to ACTION!

On the next 3 pages there are 3 Magical Mountains for you to fill in. Remember to break your big items into small doable steps, and make a date to DO THEM.

REMEMBER: climbing your Magical Mountain to reach your goal means doing **3** things:

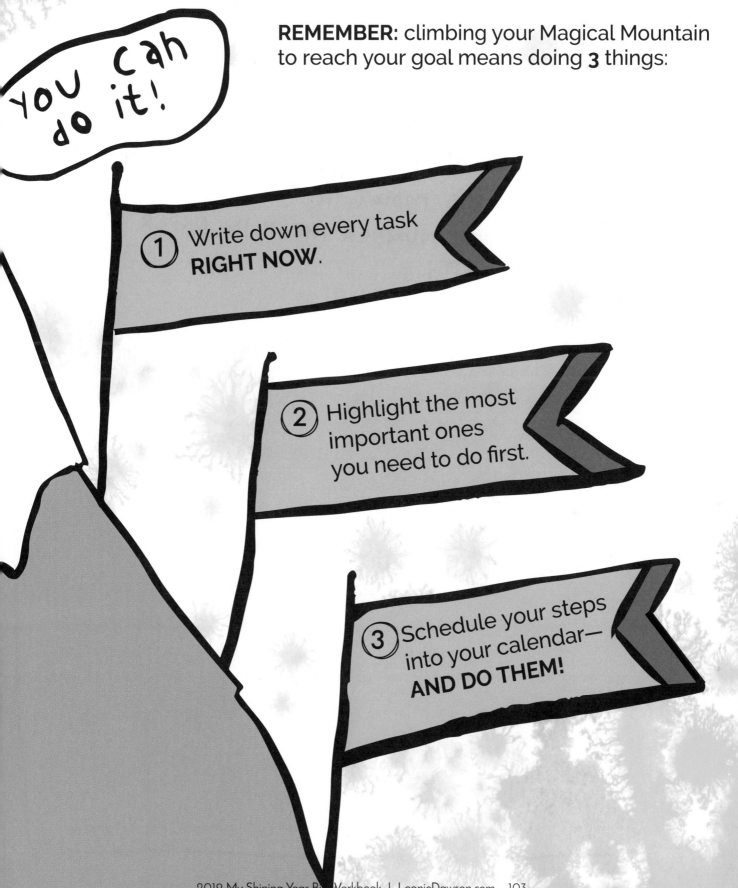

you can do it!

① Write down every task **RIGHT NOW**.

② Highlight the most important ones you need to do first.

③ Schedule your steps into your calendar— **AND DO THEM!**

magical mountain map

ADD Project Name

Write down all the steps you need to take to get up the mountain...

& THEN NUMBER THEM! IN ORDER OF PRIORITY

What support/resources do you need

FOR THIS MAGICAL MOUNTAIN TREK?
Journal what you need here:

TIME

Money

Health

Support

magical mountain map

ADD Project Name

Write down all the steps you need to take to get up the mountain...
& THEN NUMBER THEM! IN ORDER OF PRIORITY

What support/resources do you need

FOR THIS MAGICAL MOUNTAIN TREK?
Journal what you need here:

 TIME

 MONEY

 HEALTH

 Support

magical mountain map

ADD Project Name

Write down all the steps you need to take to get up the mountain...
& THEN NUMBER THEM! IN ORDER OF PRIORITY

What support/resources do you need

FOR THIS MAGICAL MOUNTAIN TREK?
Journal what you need here:

TIME

Money

Health

Support

monthly Check-ins

The stats are in, lovely.

:: 80% of people have **NO goals.**

:: 16% of people think of goals but **do NOT write them down.**

:: Just 4% of the population **write their goals down** (and by using this workbook, you're one of them! Look at you, you rare, shiny thing!)

Now here's the kicker ...

Just 1% of the population WRITE down their goals AND REGULARLY REVIEW THEM. And that 1% are among the highest achieving people in the population!

So guess what?

You're going to be one of them. At the end of every month, **have a recurring date with yourself in the calendar**. You'll check back in here and fill out that month's worksheet.

It'll keep you on track, accountable + motivated! And you'll be that incredible 1% of people who make their own dreams come true.

Juicy January

What goals did you achieve in Jan?

Any unplanned successes?

What goals will you go for in Feb?

What do you need to do to make it happen?

Fabulous February

What goals did you achieve in Feb?

Any unplanned successes?

What goals will you go for in Mar?

What do you need to do
to make it happen?

Magic March

What goals did you achieve in Mar?

Any unplanned successes?

What goals will you go for in Apr?

What do you need to do
to make it happen?

Amazing April

What goals did you achieve in Apr?

Any unplanned successes?

What goals will you go for in May?

What do you need to do to make it happen?

Marvelous May

What goals did you achieve in May?

Any unplanned successes?

What goals will you go for in Jun?

What do you need to do to make it happen?

Jubilant June

What goals did you achieve in Jun?

Any unplanned successes?

What goals will you go for in Jul?

What do you need to do to make it happen?

Joyous July

What goals did you achieve in Jul?

Any unplanned successes?

What goals will you go for in Aug?

What do you need to do
to make it happen?

Awesome August

What goals did you achieve in Aug?

Any unplanned successes?

What goals will you go for in Sep?

What do you need to do to make it happen?

Shining September

What goals did you achieve in Sep?

Any unplanned successes?

What goals will you go for in Oct?

What do you need to do to make it happen?

Over-The-Top-Terrific October

What goals did you achieve in Oct?

Any unplanned successes?

What goals will you go for in Nov?

What do you need to do to make it happen?

Nice November

What goals did you achieve in Nov?

Any unplanned successes?

What goals will you go for in Dec?

What do you need to do to make it happen?

Delish December

What goals did you achieve in Dec?

Any unplanned successes?

Time to use your 2020 workbook!

Have yourself a Very... Merry... Christmas

What To Do when you FALL OFF the WORKBOOK WAGON!

1. FORGIVE YOURSELF

2. REVIEW THIS BOOK
WHAT GOALS CAN YOU ACHIEVE THIS MONTH?

4. GO GET YOUR GOAL, GIRL!

3. GO PUBLIC
TELL FRIENDS OR YOUR MASTERMIND YOUR GOAL. ASK THEM TO HOLD YOU ACCOUNTABLE.

What is a Leonie?

Leonie Dawson is a celebrated soul-centered life + business teacher, bestselling author, and passionate philanthropist leading a multi-million-dollar company. Over the past 14 years she has taught hundreds of thousands of women how to have more spirited lives and abundant businesses.

Leonie has been recognized for her business acumen by being voted a top 6 finalist in the My Business Awards for Australian Businesswoman of the Year, and a finalist in the Ausmumpreneur of the Year Award. She is the current world record holder for the fastest person to build to the highest leadership rank in doTERRA.

Leonie lives on the Sunshine Coast in Australia with her hunky husband and their two mermaid daughters.

FACEBOOK: LeonieDawsonAuthor

WEBSITE: LeonieDawson.com

WEBSITE: ShiningYear.com

My Shining Notes

notes BRAINSTORMS + Delicious Doodling